020

START-UP
RELIGION

VISITING A MOSQUE

Ruth Nason

Evans

Published by Evans Brothers Limited
2A Portman Mansions
Chiltern Street
London W1U 6NR

© Evans Brothers Limited 2005

Produced for Evans Brothers Limited by
White-Thomson Publishing Ltd,
Bridgewater Business Centre,
210 High Street,
Lewes, East Sussex BN7 2NH

Printed in China by WKT Company Limited

Consultants: Jean Mead, Senior Lecturer in Religious
Education, School of Education, University of
Hertfordshire; Dr Anne Punter, Partnership Tutor,
School of Education, University of Hertfordshire.
Designer: Carole Binding

Cover: All photographs by Chris Fairclough

British Library Cataloguing in Publication Data
Nason, Ruth
   Visiting a mosque. - (Start-up religion)
   1. Mosques - Juvenile literature
   I. Title
   297.3'51

ISBN: 0 237 528118

Acknowledgements:
Special thanks to the following for their help and
involvement in the preparation of this book: Saadia
Durani, Dr M. Ally Soodin, the people at the Jamia
Mosque, Watford, staff and children from Peartree
Spring Junior School, Stevenage.

Picture Acknowledgements:
Corbis: pages 15 top (Dean Conger), 18 left (Suhaib
Salem/Reuters).
All other photographs by Chris Fairclough.

Contents

What is a mosque?

A mosque is a special building where Muslims go to pray. Many mosques have a dome, and a tower called a minaret.

     mosque   Muslims   pray

Musli
to do
holy k

There are five times every day when Muslims pray. Muslims can pray at home, at work, or wherever they are, but many men go to the mosque to pray together.

▲ Which words describe the inside of this mosque? Is it

dark ✳ light ✳ clean ✳ colourful ✳ calm ✳ bare ✳ beautiful?

belie

dome   minaret

Times to pray

Al

Musli
and i

A board in the mosque shows the five times of every day when Muslims must pray. The times change during the year, as the times of sunrise and sunset change.

1 Before sunrise

2 After midday

3 Mid-afternoon

▶ The second prayer time on a Friday is special, so it has its own clock on the board.

Can you
in the m

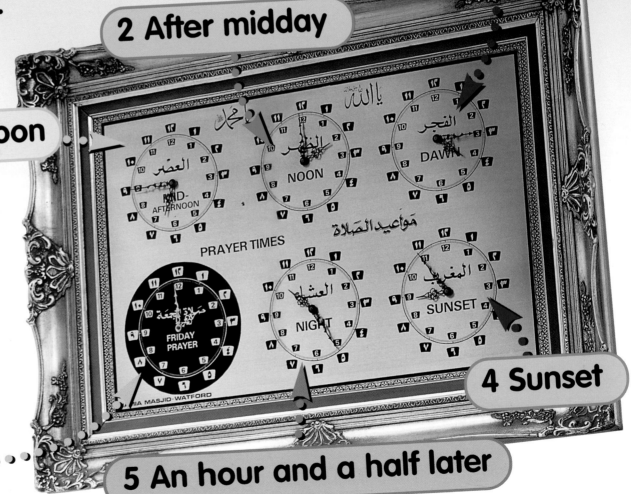

4 Sunset

5 An hour and a half later

The special prayer time on Fridays is called jumma prayer. It is a time when many Muslims go to their mosque and mosques are full of people.

◄ Before jumma prayer, the imam gives a talk about Muslim life. The imam is the man who leads the prayers in the mosque.

jumma   imam

Preparing to pray

▶ Before each prayer time, a man called a **muezzin** calls out, in Arabic, that it is time to pray. This call to prayer is called the **adhan**.

◀ When people did not have clocks or watches, muezzins called the adhan from minarets. This still happens in some countries, but not usually in Britain.

muezzin   adhan

▼ Before they pray, Muslims wash in a special way called **wudu**. They wash hands, mouth, nose, face, arms, head, ears, neck and feet three times each.

Many Muslim men and boys and all Muslim women and girls wear something on their head to pray.

wudu

Prayer positions

All over the world, when Muslims pray, they face towards a building called the Ka'aba. It stands in the Grand Mosque in Makkah, in Saudi Arabia.

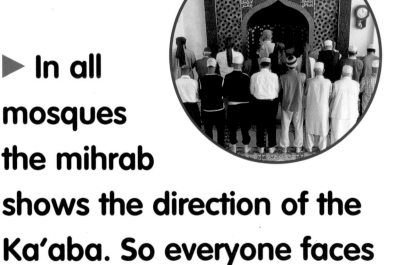

► In all mosques the mihrab shows the direction of the Ka'aba. So everyone faces the mihrab to pray.

Ka'aba   Makkah   Saudi Arabia

▼ Muslims stand on a prayer mat to pray, and repeat this set of movements called a rak'ah.

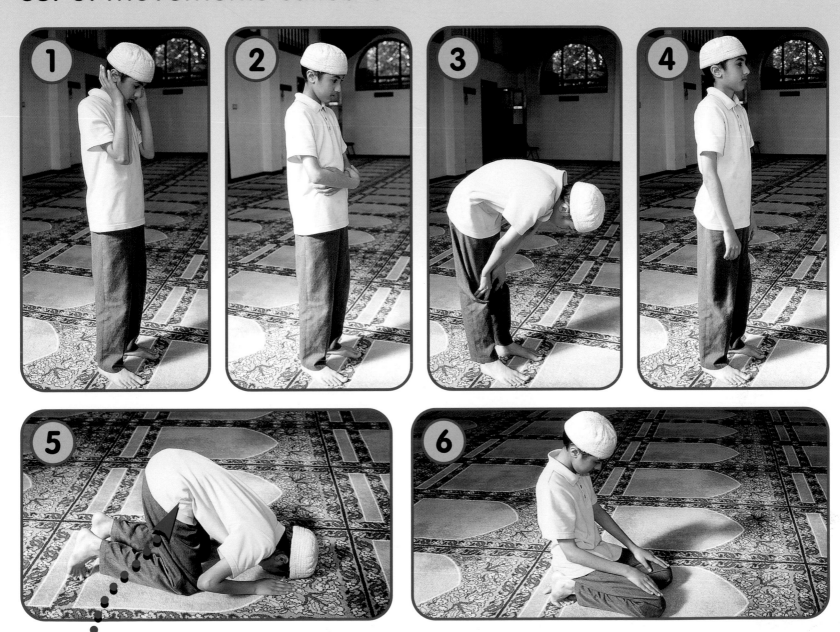

Bowing down is a way to say "I will do as Allah wants".

prayer mat   rak'ah

Learning some more

Looking at special things in the mosque helps you learn about the Muslim religion, called Islam.

▶ You will see copies of the Qur'an, and the stands that Muslims use when they read it.

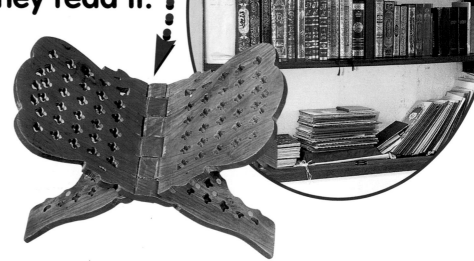

◀ You may see prayer beads that Muslims sometimes count as they say their prayers.

Islam

▶ You can also learn by talking to Muslims you meet at the mosque.

◀ Rajwan is showing how copies of the Qur'an are sometimes wrapped in cloth to protect them.

Look back at the Muslims you have seen in the mosque in this book. What questions would you like to ask them?

Further information for

New words introduced in the text:

adhan	dome	jumma	muezzin	Prophet	worship
alcove	gallery	Ka'aba	Muslims	Muhammad	wudu
Allah	God	Makkah	peace	Qur'an	
Arabia	headscarf	messengers	pray	rak'ah	
Arabic	holy book	mihrab	prayer beads	respect	
believe	imam	minaret	prayer mat	Saudi Arabia	
decorated	Islam	mosque	prayer times	tiles	

Background Information

Pages 4-5: Mosque is the English word for *Masjid*, a Muslim place of worship. Traditionally this incorporates a dome, originally designed for good acoustics and air circulation, and a minaret for the call to prayer. Some mosques in Britain have been adapted from other buildings and so may not have these features. Mosques also serve as community centres.
The prayer hall is used for the five daily prayers. Muslims arriving to pray stand shoulder to shoulder in rows, starting from the centre front. It is forbidden for women to pray in front of men, as it is considered immodest and distracting, and so a separate gallery or room is usually provided. Prayers may be performed anywhere, on a clean place or prayer mat.

Pages 6-7: Muslims believe the Qur'an to contain the actual words of Allah, revealed to the Prophet Muhammad by the Angel Gabriel in Arabic. The Qur'an is always learned in that language. The Qur'an is treated with respect and not normally put on the floor or on laps. The Qur'an and Arabic books and cards open the opposite way to books in English.
The after-school class is called a madrasah.

Pages 8-9: The Prophet Muhammad is regarded as the last of the prophets. He is never worshipped or thought divine, and it is inappropriate to call Muslims 'Mohammedans'. Everything known about the Prophet Muhammad is called the *Sunnah*, and Muslims use this as a source of guidance about life and practice. Collections of reports of the words and actions of the Prophet, known as the *Hadith*, are a part of the *Sunnah*. In English writing, Muslims use the abbreviation 'p.b.u.h.' (peace be upon him) after the Prophet Muhammad's name. Muslims also respect other biblical prophets, including Jesus (*Isa*) and Moses (*Musa*).

Pages 10-11: Above the *mihrab* is the *Shahadah*, the basic Muslim statement of faith. When leading prayers the *imam* faces into the *mihrab*. The 'steps' in the photograph on page 11 are a pulpit for the Friday sermon (see page 15).

Pages 12-13: When preparing for a visit observe the appropriate etiquette. As shoes will be removed, ask children to have clean socks. Females should have a headscarf, and women should wear loose, modest clothing. In the mosque, avoid sitting with feet pointing towards the *mihrab*.

Parents and Teachers

Pages 14-15: The prayers said five times daily are called *salat*. They last about five minutes and are followed by personal prayer called *dua*. The prayers may be performed 'in arrears' if it has not been possible to do them in the right time-slot. Friday is not a 'day of rest', but Muslim men are required to pray in congregation for the Friday 'after-midday' prayers if possible. (The top photo on page 15 shows Friday prayers at the Sultan Mosque, Singapore.)

Pages 16-17: The 'd' in the words *adhan* and *wudu* is sometimes pronounced as if it is combined with a 'z'.

Pages 18-19: The *Ka'aba* is the focus of the *Hajj* pilgrimage, which commemorates the story of Ibrahim. The direction for prayer can be found using a special *qiblah* compass.

Pages 20-21: The Qur'an is usually kept on the highest shelf and placed on a stand to read. It is only handled after *wudu*. The prayer beads are called *tasbih* and are often used for personal prayers before or after the *salat*. There are usually 99 beads, divided into three sets of 33 for reciting 'Glory be to Allah', 'Thanks be to Allah' and 'Allah is great'.

Suggested Activities

■ Show pictures of a range of mosque buildings, and discuss what makes them mosques (use/design?).

■ Visit a local mosque or use a virtual visit.

■ Make thankyou cards after a visit, by sticking on gold-coloured dome and minaret shapes.

■ Read some stories about the Prophet Muhammad, and other prophets mentioned in the Qur'an.

■ Make some calligraphy of the name of Allah by tracing or doing rubbings from plaques (link to Art NC 2c). How many

Books and Websites

My Muslim Faith (Big Book), Khadijah Knight, Evans, 1999
Muslim Artefacts Teaching Pack, Vida Barnett, Articles of Faith, 1995
Stories of the Prophets (6 board books), Siddiqa Juma, Iman, 1999
Teaching RE – Islam 5-11, CEM, 1997

RE 'gateway' sites provide recommendations for videos and books and links to organisations, sources of artefacts and other useful websites for teachers and pupils.

http://re-xs.ucsm.ac.uk – links to sites on Islam
http://theredirectory.org.uk – links to Muslim organisations
http://www.theresite.org.uk – links to 18 KS1 sites on Islam and to virtual tours of mosques such as
http://www.hitchams.suffolk.sch.uk/mosque/default.htm

times can children recognise the word in this book, or on a mosque visit? Let children make and decorate 'calligraphy' of their own names, using outlined letters produced by ICT or two pencils banded together. Discuss the importance of names.

■ Make tessellating patterns. (Link to Maths 'repeating patterns in 2D shapes' and Art NC 3b.)

■ Listen to the call to prayer, prayers or verses from the Qur'an being recited in Arabic (tape, video or on a visit).

■ Talk about the value of preparing for something very special.

■ Look at and find out about some Muslim artefacts, treating them with appropriate respect.

■ Ask a Muslim child or visitor to tell about what *salat* and the mosque mean to him, or use a video clip.

Index